THE MARVELOUS BONES OF TIME

THE MARVELOUS BONES OF TIME

Excavations and Explanations

POETRY BY

Brenda Coultas

COFFEE HOUSE PRESS
MINNEAPOLIS

COPYRIGHT © 2007 Brenda Coultas
COVER ART "Born Lost" © Robert McDaniel
AUTHOR PHOTOGRAPH © Bob Gwaltney
COVER + BOOK DESIGN Linda S. Koutsky

COFFEE HOUSE PRESS books are available to the trade through our primary distributor, Consortium Book Sales & Distribution, www.cbsd.com or (800) 283-3572. For personal orders, catalogs, or other information, write to: Coffee House Press, 27 North Fourth Street, Suite 400, Minneapolis, MN 55401.

COFFEE HOUSE PRESS is a nonprofit literary publishing house. Support from private foundations, corporate giving programs, government programs, and generous individuals helps make the publication of our books possible. We gratefully acknowledge their support in detail in the back of this book.

To you and our many readers around the world, we send our thanks for your continuing support.

LIBRARY OF CONGRESS CIP INFORMATION
Coultas, Brenda.
The Marvelous bones of time : excavations and explanations / by Brenda Coultas.
p. cm.
ISBN-13: 978-1-56689-204-9
ISBN-10: 1-56689-204-X
I. Title.
PS3603.O886M37 2007   811'.6—DC22   2007021003

FIRST EDITION | FIRST PRINTING
1 3 5 7 9 8 6 4 2

ACKNOWLEDGMENTS
Thanks are due to the many editors of journals, web sites and anthologies where some of these poems first appeared: *Absent One, Bombay Gin, Conjunctions, Court Green, Columbia Review, Denver Quarterly, Encyclopedia, Explosive, Fascicle, Insurance, Poetry Project Newsletter, Rebel Road, Skanky Possum, Swerve, Yawp.*

I wish to thank New York Foundation for the Arts and the Lower Manhattan Cultural Council for providing time and space in which to write.

THE ABOLITION JOURNAL (OR TRACING THE EARTHWORKS OF MY COUNTY) — I wish to thank Bob Gwaltney, Mark Coomer, and Dr. Randy Mills for sharing their research into abolitionist activity in Southwestern Indiana. This is a relativity undocumented field where the remaining sites of underground railroad activity are still largely unprotected from further destruction. I wish to thank those who listened: Marcella Durand, Tonya Foster, Elenia Gamin, Robert McDaniel, Eleni Sikelianos, and Jo Ann Wasserman.

A LONELY CEMETERY — My gratitude to those who generously shared their stories with me: Dave Brinks, Liz Castanga, Elaine Coultas, Kenneth and Kim Coultas, Valerie Deus, Melissa Goodrum, Alice B. Talkless, Timothy Yearby, Donald and Juanita Yearby, Mitch Highfill, Kim Lyons, Nathaniel Siegel, and David Vogan. And to thank the magic pens of Eleni Sikelianos, Marcella Durand, Tonya Foster, Jo Ann Wasserman, and Elania Gamin. I'm indebted to Simon Pettet for sharing his insights into the paranormal. I am deeply and happily indebted to Robert McDaniel, my co-investigator and collaborator in "The Robert Investigations." Thank you to Atticus Fierman for generously and patiently supporting this work. Thank you to Michael Leigh, Scott and Susie Gerth for an evening of tales of the uncanny.

THE MARVELOUS BONES OF TIME

CONTENTS

BOOK I

THE ABOLITION JOURNAL
(or, Tracing the Earthworks of My County)

"The Iroquois called the river 'Ohio' and the name was later translated by the French as 'the Beautiful—La Belle Riviere.' Not a beautiful river, mind you, but the beautiful, with no fear that it might be confused with any other."

—OHIO RIVER MUSEUM WEB SITE,
MARIETTA, OHIO

CONTENTS

"He is from the north where they
are all lying, thieving abolitionists."

—FROM WILLIAM COCKRUM'S
The Underground Railroad

"The very state where grew the bread
That formed my bones, I see"

—ABE LINCOLN

The Abolition Journal
(or, Tracing the Earthworks of My County)

I found pathways and markers but none led directly north
I could walk and find an arrowhead or spear point
I could walk after the plowing and find flints
I knew someone, an ironworker, who could point out burial
    and village sites in the river bottoms

These things can be proven with stone

I could follow these paths and find car bodies and dump sites
deer bones and garbage

I could mow a new path; still, it would not be evidence
Even if the tobacco leaves all pointed north, it would not
    be evidence.

I never worked or floated a boat on the Anderson River or ferried anyone across the Ohio. I did not walk to Gentryville to borrow a book or to repay two cents. I did not move to Illinois to practice law. I was not in love with Ann Rutledge nor Joshua Speed and I did not marry Mary Todd although I have always admired her. No, I have never split a rail and indeed I am not a Republican.

Looking from the free state
there is a river then a slave state
Turn around and there is a slave state,
a river
then a free state

I was born between the free side and the slave side, my head crowning on the bridge. I fully emerged in an elevator traveling upward in a slave state. I have shopped in the slave state and eaten barbecue there. I have walked along the riverbank in the slave state and looked out at a free state.

Lincoln looked out over the river and saw a slave state and he was born in one (Kentucky), like me, but was raised in a free state (Indiana), like me. We were white and so could cross the river.

Question: are there any abolitionists hanging from my family tree?

Riding a yellow school bus through Lincoln City
Are other Hoosiers, the residents of Spencer county, thinking of
    Lincoln?

I was a Midway Panther   Chrisney Wildcat   Heritage Hills Patriot
Surrounded in all directions by
Tell City Marksmen
South Spencer Rebels
Tecumseh Braves
Boonville Pioneers
New Harmony Rappites (Utopians), and I used to call myself an
    American.

I (am a color that is an uneven beige; have a face with reddish tones) read about a man who is described as colored and free

If, in the document, she is described as an old darky, then I might be described as an old whitey

I am the gelatinous mass that surrounds the yolk

Some of these places I knew the names of:

Diamond Island is an island I have seen from the bridge

Wabash River, I swam in

Peabody Coal Mines, formerly cornfields; I might have been
      drunk there

The documents describe a fisherman's hut

they describe a bank and a point

they describe a river

they pretend their business is bass, perch, bluegill

which they sell to steam- and flatboats

and they travel at night up Little Pigeon Creek, from which my
      father fished

The engineer conducted a train
regularly he (colored)
and free
the silent train
riders (of what color?)
moving toward water

the train has a head and runs through the night
the length and carriage of it
trees and crops fly by

driving through a finger of water
over the shoulders of a river
into the mouth of a creek
toward a point on shore

put this in your pocket to confuse the bloodhounds
when you are moving toward a point in the distance across water
which divides countries

moving to a point or to point out over here or there
there is a shore or woods, then someone points and makes a place

travel by night and let no one see you

in a matter of tracking a passage through grass, how difficult after
100 or more years

A historian wrote: "Miss Delia S. Webster was known to have helped slaves across into Indiana, especially south of Jeffersonville."

He is Known to be a slave catcher and hunter
He is Known to be sympathetic to Kentucky
He is Known to be a liar

A hundred years hence, will there be markers commemorating where we had borrowed a book? Will there be symbols pointing out our former dwellings and facsimiles of our living rooms? Will our belongings be preserved; the childhood books and clothes, journals and cursive handwriting? And if the original is missing, will they write "this is similar to . . . ," or "this is of the period" ?

From the tobacco warehouse, Old Uncle Simon led others out, saying "freedom would do him no good now."

Me, a blade of Grass Township
Spencer County
Southern Indiana.

I thought of klansmen when I thought of Indiana, I thought of
the Imperial Wizard Stephenson, forty miles to my west, and so
I thought to know what is better about the folks of my county.

    Southern sympathies travel over water.
    Only in my forty-seventh year did I know I was a Yankee

Hoosier: a backwards person: a frontier corruption of who's your
daddy?

THE EXECUTIVES OF THE ANTI-SLAVERY LEAGUE
IN NEIGHBORING COUNTIES:

Ira Caswell's was the first station in Warrick county. His family
said, "a lone tree
from his orchard still standing," and "the traces of his home-
stead," and asked
Peabody Coal to preserve this abolitionist's farm
(and of which we await the coalbreath's answer)

And did there exist Col. William Cockrum's
Oakland City station as the plaque suggests?
(the 21st-century mayor's late 20th-century house rests on the site)

Did Dr. Posey's coal bank,
shelter passengers guided by stars?
(who chomped-up this site, Black Beauty or Peabody Coal?)

"The President" of this railroad, Levi Coffin of Wayne County,
too far north to count in my poem.

When he writes "the body is ironed," he means leg irons and a large iron ball.

EMANCIPATION PROCLAMATION

If I said "Emancipation" or if it said "Manumitted" in this
county, if I said
"Reparations" (some might say those are fighting words)

or if I said "Lyles Station," the first black town in Gibson
County, or I could say
"Stevenson Station," a black settlement within shouting distance
of the South
in Vanderburgh County, and I could say Lincoln Gardens (a
historic housing project in Evansville).

In the history of the county, they wrote Co. for colored.

Of Lyles Station in 1849

I could certainly write "the best cantaloupes in these sandy bot-
     toms," and

"the first African Methodist Episcopal church."

I could write "a station existed run by a freeman Thomas Cole."

I could write "these nearby whites

David Stormont

John Caithers

David Hull

assisted passengers."

I could write, "the author of *Lyles Station Yesterday and Today* asks why this history has been left out of the textbooks."

The palmist heard many voices, a mournful ocean coming from
my right hand
And felt a deep sadness.

She heard,
"I went to the underworld and this is what I found"
She heard,
"I have her body."

Then I heard the word and the word was "Autonomy."

Born ninety-three years after
My mother born in Indiana sixty-two years after
Her mother born in Kentucky 1896
Her mother born in Kentucky, and during her lifetime
The first grandchild born 121 years after the news of
    Emancipation

A Poultice from a Coultas

In tracing a passage through grass, lacking physical evidence
I turn to the language of

A dark horse   A horse of a different color

Stop Horsing around
Hold your Horses
Flogging a dead Horse
Rode hard and put up wet
Chomping at the bit
Oh, Horse hockey!

Shake a leg, y'all being helped on? Money burning a hole in your
pocket (when my grandpa said this, a dollar was a slug of silver)

Whoa nellie whoa   Quit skylarking around
I'll jerk a knot in your tail

Barn door's open and the horse is getting out

Soon I was writing in the language of horse-drawn days

Here apply this to your sore tooth it's a
poultice from a Coultas

shove it in your crown of burly leaves
I can find better use for tobacco   make a doily for the arms of

chairs even though tobacco plates leave a tar ring

                                                   I've churned their words
count on your chickens that are hatching or all resting in one basket
get your bacon caught in a ringer
like a mule at a trough or a silk ear stolen from a sow's purse

I'm sorting needles in the sun while the haystack still shines

We sang, "she'll be coming around the mountain when she comes," and of the old cotton fields back home, but we have neither mountains nor cotton fields. We have tobacco worms, tomato worms, tumble bugs, and june bugs

She'll be riding six white horses when she comes she'll be riding six white horses when she comes   in reality we ride one angry white barrel-chested pony

the books from the old house, which I took with me because I need another language

                                                Who read *The Carpetbagger?*

"Take your shoes off at the bridge," my grandpa said, "We're entering Kentucky."

There was a war between the Kentuckians and the Hoosiers. The Kentuckians were throwing firecrackers and the Hoosiers were lighting them and throwing them back.

There was a Hoosier fishing on one bank and a Kentuckian fishing on the other. The Hoosier was catching lots of fish while the Kentuckian had none. The Kentuckian said "I'm not getting any bites over here." The Hoosier said "Come over and try this side, I'll shine my flashlight beam and you can walk over on it." The Kentuckian said, "No way, I'll get halfway there and you'll turn it off."

Have you heard about the new state farm?
They put a fence around Kentucky.

Why do ducks fly upside down over Kentucky?
There's nothing worth shitting on.

Do you know why they built a bridge across the Ohio River?
So Kentuckians can swim across in the shade.

Although it is called the Bluegrass State, they are better known for their weed. You can buy any kind of drug in most factory parking lots.

There are drive-thru liquor stores and dry counties in Kentucky.

They have bluegrass music and a radio show called Old Scratchy Records. Bill Monroe and the Shady Boys lived there.

Daniel Boone brought the first slaves to Kentucky.

Kentuckians roller-skate in old tobacco barns and frequent the "World's Largest Thrift Shop" on Twenty-second Street in Louisville.

Everyone strips tobacco in Kentucky. They know barbecue and horses in Kentucky.

Wendell Berry, a poet, is from Kentucky.
The Shakers built a round barn in Kentucky.

For heaven's sake, Kentucky is all that separates us from Tennessee.

My husband tells everyone we are going to Kentucky because people get very excited about this idea called Kentucky.

I was the secretary of the Owensboro Junior Coin club in Kentucky.

Johnny Depp and Richard Hell went to high school in Kentucky.

I attended the reburial of 600 Native American graves at Slack Farm in Kentucky.

I've never been to Rough River nor Goldie's Opera House in Owensboro, Kentucky.

There is a Paris, Illinois and a Paris, Kentucky.

Lily Tomlin and Bobbie Ann Manson are from Paducah, Kentucky. Ashley Judd is from Ashville, Kentucky.

There are underground coal mines in Kentucky and strip mines in Indiana. I like the strong labor unions of Kentucky where everyone sits on porches.

W.C. Handy gave birth to the blues in Henderson, Kentucky where they fought to keep the Super Wal-Mart out.

John James Audubon lived with his slaves in the wilds of Kentucky.
Josiah Henson escaped from Yellowbanks, Kentucky.

Edgar Cayce and bell hooks are from Beverly, Kentucky.
I stayed at Land Between the Lakes once, a huge man-made lake in a dry county, famous for its prison in Kentucky.

Thomas Merton prayed in Kentucky.
I had my collarbone set in Kentucky.
My mother had a hysterectomy in Kentucky.

I know a man who calls it K-wacky because brothers and sisters
and first cousins marry each other in Kentucky.

They grow their fingernails long and gouge out eyes. They bite off
ears and lips in barroom brawls in Kentucky.

Disclaimer: I am sorry about all the beans I spilled on Kentucky.
Some of my family members and friends are from Kentucky.

THE OLD SLAVE HOUSE IN ILLINOIS,
A FREE STATE

Crossing the Walbash, above the Ohio, traveling through a free state, we came to a red mansion with a hidden carriage entrance, an attic of cells, and a whipping post. The guide showed us a cast iron cylinder made to cover a slave's penis.

The owner John Hart Crenshaw kidnapped freed black men and women to work in his salt mine and then resold them into slavery.

He ferried them across in the darkness to Kentucky.

A Postcard

The reverse side is inscribed "abolitionist." I know this to be true as I have read her mighty speeches, and I know she is a woman, too. This occurred in Indiana where she had to bare her breasts. I never doubted her, and when she said, "Ain't I a woman, too?" I said "Yes," from this place in which I write, and in which she once lived, and there exists a library named for her and as always, we are near a river.

In My Township

Come to Grass Township where very few smoke the grass, oh,
they might smoke cornsilk, jimson weed, crystal meth, or chew
tobacco in their grasshopper mouths

The old plat book with names written in spidery ink, *McCoy,*
    Cruz, Ash, Gwaltney,
Plots of land divied up by the first white men

    This grass alley by my cousin's is called Circadian Lane

The last outhouse is behind the church, but I drop my drawers
    anywhere in the woods

"You're nothing but a little pill," said my Grandpa Yearby

Bushel of wheat
bushel of rye
all for Midway holler I

Once I knew a girl whose initials were K.K.K. and her two sisters
were named after spices
Grasshoppers spit out tobacco, I hate their mouths

What do you think this is, your birthday, Coatless?

You're so buck toothed you look like you could eat an ear of corn through a picket fence.

A Place of Bread and Milk

Candy case, cash register embossed with curlicues, all the cent and dollar amounts pop up in the window: the wooden change drawer, the adding machine's black body with ivory-and-red keys. The soda cooler where the drinks stood in water. An upright woodburner, not a potbellied stove: spittoons, brass and fancy, or an empty tin can will do.

In 1976 I went to the store to pick up
milk
bread
grape juice
saltines
milk of magnesia
jelly

Bloomfield, Midway, Sandridge, Enterprise, Fulda, Jonesboro, Eureka, New Boston, Rockport, Hatfield, Evanston, Buffaloville, Santa Claus, Pueblo, Pyeattville, French Island, Lincoln City, St. Meinrad, Mariah Hill, Lamar

                              No, I have not been everywhere
But I've been around
even to Bullocktown (Warrick County)

Although the post office closed in 1895
I mailed a letter

A post office once but every store was.
When we tear this building down, what will be found?
Hidden love letters?
Lost buttons or wedding bands?
Square-head nails or wooden spikes?
Silver dollars, with Liberty walking in full stride?

Under the Rockport bluff, a plaque noting the cave of the first white family in the county, of Tecumseh Lankford who begat Bloomfield once called Tippecanoe once called Yearbyville after my mother's family because a plethora of Yearbys once lived there.

Every white man aimed his gun at Tecumseh, Shawnee for shooting star. Daniel Grass, the first white property owner in this township, his family killed by arrows.

Spier Spencer died at Tippecanoe, a battlefield far from here, yet they gave this county his name.

In 1812, every white man said "Tippecanoe, too."

A Jar of Tomatoes Canned Forty Years Ago
Waits to Be Opened

My cousin and I pointed out where a house used to be and we pointed to a row of sandstone boulders that marked the boundary. We pointed and said there was an oak there and the church held services underneath it. In this patch of weeds, there was a brick schoolhouse, then there were hogs and the hogs lived in the old school, and then it was weeds and the hogs lived in the weeds. Now there are no hogs, only weeds.

The chicken house always stood alone

This place had a summer kitchen
two rooms wrapped in brown tarpaper

The last one standing is white
This one had magazines and an electric light to read by
We spoke romantically of outhouses

"Here," we pointed, "they showed movies in the barn."

"Here," we said, "some children tore down this house just to see what was underneath, to find a silver dime and log foundation. That house passed into fiction."

Pointing, we said, "there was a house there, in front of the trailers, and we found hidden love letters written by the old man."

That was not a house
There was not a house   that was always a field
This double-wide tops a fruit cellar

Under my pillow, stone axes and ornaments: the first man-made
     things.
Are the stars above the oldest elements in the county?

Buffaloville

I want to live in Buffaloville and have all my letters postmarked
Buffaloville and spend only buffalo head nickels
Silver, the tuft of hair under the buffalo belly

There are no buffalo in Buffaloville
no Lincolns in Lincoln City,
no Santa Claus in Christmas Lake Village
very few Indians in Indiana

The preface to my family history reads, "there is very little, if any, published about this family or the branches that follow." In searching for a trace in a great-grandfather, born in 1865, Grayson County, at the end of the Civil War in the divided state of Kentucky, to be named William Sherman. A Republican and a Baptist, signs of Northern sympathies.

Although white, were they following the North Star?

About the sins and crimes of Indiana, I'd rather talk about my
    neighbor.
I was born fifty-eight years after the lynching of three in the
    county seat.

The courthouse, thrice built, three stories under a stained glass rotunda; the crown jewel of the county.

COAL SEAMS UNDER THE CORN FIELDS

I ask my brother if there were arrowheads
flints
TV antennas to be found?
And did he take his son to search
junker cars in the woods
Or for the shards of our ancestors in
blue Vick's VapoRub or
Ball jars
or white Pond's cold cream jars buried behind the pond?

Kentucky, a slice off Virginia
Spencer County, a slice of Perry and Warrick

Towns once named for nature now named for men:
Chrisney was Springs Station
Henderson was Red Banks
Owensboro was Yellow Banks
Evansville, Crescent City, for the bend of the river.
Hatfield was called Fair Fight.
Do they fight fair in Hatfield? I'll ask my cousin who lives there.

Of this name, Iroquois is not the only one   the Shawnee said
Kis-ke-ba-la-se-pe (Eagle river)
Wyandottes said O-he-zuh-yean-de-wa,
Delawares said "Pal-a-wa-the-pec"
Each nation giving its own name

Africa, in the river bottoms, north bank, washed away. No evidence, barely written down. I asked if this was a settlement of freed people? The librarian can tell me
nothing   only the name remains.

Emancipation Day observed on September 22 in the twentieth century.

"... the Hoosier state stands alone before the world unwilling that the native born citizens of the United States, with a colored skin, shall attempt to earn an honest living within her limits."

A black woman cursed that she would reach into the past for the slavemaster's whip

As we land, the only African American passenger on board tells us he was born and raised in Los Angeles and brought his family to Kentucky to visit friends, and they refused to leave. He plans on commuting to see his family every vacation until his retirement from the post office in a few years. "Owensboro," he said. "Heaven," he said.

Two Cabins

Josiah's Cabin
—Owensboro, Kentucky

Driving down Frederica Street, I think of how to get to the mall and not of the buffalo who made this road. Not of the street's namesake, Frederica, daughter of Tippecanoe war hero Rossboro, in this town that was once called Yellow Banks / Rossoboro / Owensborough and the home of Ragu Spaghetti Sauce and the site of the last public execution.

Going for a walk in that peculiar institution; up the hill, there are fields and a farmhouse not old enough to be Amos Riley's plantation. On the bottom, a valley. Not many miles before the house where a teenage Abe was acquitted of operating a ferry without a license. We look for the foundation of a cabin and find not a sandstone to be turned over, and think of the skiff, the journey across water. Landing in Grandview moving east toward Ohio with his family of five; two babies hidden in a knapsack and carried 200 miles. A pioneer woman gave him meat tied up in cloth.

Josiah Henson (a model for *Uncle Tom's Cabin*)
Founder of Dawn, a utopia for fugitive slaves.
Later, his visage on a Canadian postage stamp.
Knighted yet best known for his grave betrayal.

ABE'S CABIN

—LINCOLN CITY, INDIANA

Walking on the free side, in this town once called Kercheval, the original stones mark a trail. Faux cabin and outbuildings. A bronze casting of the hearth of Tom Lincoln's cabin. A faux pioneer spins wool.

Milk sickness   his mother's grave   the largest stone of all.

First crop corn   spicebush sassafras persimmon

His sister rests in Little Pigeon cemetery behind the thrice built and named church: Little Pigeon Meeting House / Old Pigeon church / New Pigeon

IN A GAZE

Of what I learned in gazing
not at a crystal ball
but at the surface of water

of what I learned in gazing
Southern sympathies traveled across water.

of what I learned in gazing into an abyss or river
of how difficult to see into a body

of what I learned in gazing
a wolf is a Northern who captures runaways
of freedom names
of sleeper cells of abolition

from the bluffs of Rockport once called Hanging Rock.
of violence in a body
of either water or flesh
of complicity and of resistance

What did I learn about my kinfolk?
Petroglyphs mostly
divided as the bluegrass

Of this branch planted in Kentucky, Simon Pryor owned three
    people:

Of this same fork, Hiram Harris, a Unionist, of the Third Cavalry
    volunteers.
Injured his back in Siege of Corinth, and still marched with
    Sherman to the sea.

Seeking benefits as a Civil War widow, my great-great-grand-
    mother wrote that she has not aided or abetted the rebellion
    in the United States.

Gazing at the spiderlegged ink

rough crazy quilt   I thought to loosen it all, to pull the thread
    let the rags fall

Arriving by air
gazing at the blue and grays
bordered by shiny thread
elaborate chicken scratchings

the patchworked land below us
parcels of land enscribed in the plat book of 1815
a European geometry imposed on native curves
the black and white pages of the plat book animated into color

BOOK II

A LONELY CEMETERY

1. What are the confusing incidents of the story?
2. What are the amusing incidents of the story?
3. Is the author intentionally confusing and amusing?
4. What is the climax of the story?
5. Is the story possible?

—HANDWRITTEN BY JIMMY JONES
ON THE FLYLEAF OF
Prose and Poetry for Appreciation (1935)

CONTENTS

PART IV —
SPIRIT TOLD ME

Every word you are about to read is true
or believed to be so.

PART I
A LONELY CEMETERY

"Have you seen the ghost of Tom, long white bones with the flesh all gone, oooo, oooo, wouldn't it be chilly with no skin on."

My friend,

Much has been said and there is——much talk about the glories of heaven and its enjoyment. But think now all of the splendor of the etherial world could——the soul for the separation from or the loss of its loved ones no dear friend it is the knowledge that it can return bringing the sweet love and wisdom which it has gathered from the like divine that makes the souls heaven to know and be known to love, and to be loved, to be assured that even——all will be gathered into the immortal heritage. This is indeed heaven all else is but the——of manifestation of——like to teach you friend.

—Thomas Gray [a disembodied spirit]

Dear Mom and Dad,

How are you? I know you are all right because spirit told me so in Fox cottage. Mom, you have a guide named Rising Sun, and I have a guide whose part of name is Panda. I am feeling alright. Oh yes. Please send receipt for express ticket of trunk and box. May God Bless You All

—Helen

I will only say this about the dream to keep it short. Some spider like monster tried to get at me by smashing some appendage through the roof of a white car I was in. The dream turned to another event about a big brown bear on top of a clear dome. There was evergreen trees and land and daylight inside. The bears teeth was trying to twist the metal frame to get in. It had only got through some clear plastic. Then I heard a voice in the dream say, "don't worry it can't get in." Then I got up from the dream.

—From a letter addressed to the Parapsychology Association

I asked the cards if my poem would be successful. The reader said, "Who is that man with the dark glasses and pot belly? Is there any reason why I should be seeing Allen Ginsberg over your shoulder?"

A Lonely Cemetery
—After a line by Pablo Neruda

There is a lonely cemetery outside my window, but no one gets buried there anymore. I mean that you would have had to have died a hundred years earlier. A living man I know has been inside the tombs and says the dead are encased in leather and sitting upright awaiting the final days. Some lie inside talking, while others' lips are covered with moss.

There are lonely cemeteries and there are cemeteries that wish to be alone so they send out ghosts. Late at night I visit paranormal web sites and listen to the recordings of disembodied voices and watch videos of spirit orbs. Look at this one of a man with an ectoplasm vortex surrounding him. Listen to this recording from Custer's battlefield; you can hear the whoosh of tomahawks slicing the air.

We went to where everyone saw them, but we got scared and fled. Looked in the battlefields where sorrows had occurred, and sometimes we felt them there. Walked in the woods and read inscriptions on the monuments placed at the site of great carnage. Looked in the skeletons of houses, in attics and boxes and prairies too. In the grasses, in the meadows, to where bullets, turned soft blue and gray, are still found.

Reburial

Wood Lawn Cemetery in the Bronx is where the Four Train goes directly but slowly to its death, is resurrected and sent back to Manhattan.

We could make a home out of this temple; it's roomy but cold. This one is simple and tasteful. The one with the pebbles placed on top is our neighbor Melville. This tomb is mine, although it is shaped like a tenement apartment, not the Cheops Pyramid, or the Woolworth crypt even though it is also shotgun-shaped and overpriced.

The building and carving of stone
the laying out of the lines
did all the work myself

        although I currently reside here not after.

The Tear in the Fabric between Time and Space

They asked us if we wanted our room haunted or not, so we took the haunted one hoping for evidence. When it came, I pulled the covers up over my head and prayed it would go away. When it came to my husband, during a nocturnal bathroom visit, he closed his eyes and ran back to bed.

At breakfast other guests said they heard crashing noises all night like the sound of pots and pans banging. We heard nothing but the cook's radio playing heavy metal. Here's some advice: stay away from restaurants advertising "original battlefield food."

During the tour, a guide told us about the hole in the fabric between time and space. It goes like this: A woman took a picture of a remodeled house, but on film the house appeared exactly as it did during the battle, without siding or an electric porch light. Or, this example, when crossing a small ditch in town some tourists have felt a tug on their pant legs, by the ghosts of soldiers who drowned there. They say that because of the hole President Eisenhower prowls the upstairs of the post office, once his summer White House. Later, in the bar, for further proof of the time and space tear, the guide showed us a photograph a guest sent of a white vapor hovering over the bedspread. Now that's quite a tear in the fabric of time and space.

Neighborhood monsters leave muddy footprints larger than a man's and are hairy with red eyes and a distinct odor; they live in the woods and can be found loping across the pasture at dusk. At one time, everyone was worried about the Hatfield Monster, and some had seen him at the edge of the woods on Silverdale Road. So we locked the doors and gunned the engine when we drove by.

I can count our monsters on one hand: the Spottsville Monster by the Spottsville Dam in Kentucky, the Bloomington Bigfoot in Monroe County, and the giant catfish, larger than the length of a full-grown man, that feed at the locks of the Newburgh Dam in Newburgh, Indiana.

No one has caught any of them, although there are web sites dedicated to proving their existence. Hmmm, a whole belt of them in Ohio. These monsters leave no bodies, no burrows or caves, only theories and a few lone witnesses. Would the catfish leave us a whisker to measure? A swim bladder or bone?

Perry County, where my dad grew up, has lots of caves where he found arrowheads and a rock called Indian chalk that you can write in red with. He never mentioned a monster to us.

What about the tiny monster in our pond that lived in the mud and sent out red feelers, and when we brushed it with sticks, it drew back? No name for it, an unrecorded species without a theory and with only children as witnesses. When we took it out of the water, it was merely mud.

I fished, trying to sink my line down to the bottom feeders, try-
ing to find the bed of the pond, trying to guess how deep the
water and how strange those animals might be. I built cages, out
of wire and sticks, to contain them. When I caught one, I worked
hard to bring him home (he was heavy with claws and had a great
bite) and to build an escape-proof pen. I put the monster in, put
in grass and corn for his dinner, put chicken wire over the top
with a ten-pound stone to secure it
felt confident
slept well that night and returned in the morning.
Opened the lid
stuck a pole in
fished around
nada
nothing.
He had escaped under cover of darkness.

I remember wanting to find a new species or a rare animal. My
sister saw a bobcat eating Soybean Saint, our dead pony who was
rotting in the woods, but I prefer to remember riding him with
five of us on his back and a wreath of daisies around his neck.

Disclaimer: During the writing of this work, which began 40
years ago, some animals died but most of them escaped.

A True Account of When We Lived in a Haunted House

When I was a full-time welder and a part-time fashion model, I lived on the second floor of a haunted mansion with my sister. From the street, the house appeared to be abandoned. It was a three-story brick building with heavy shrubs and rotting gutters, one block from the river in an old Victorian neighborhood, half ghetto and half old money, where riverboat captains of the nineteenth century had once lived in gilded splendor. Their mansions had been chopped up into tiny and sometimes bizarre apartments and were owned by one slumlord who pounded his property signs into the weak grass.

Our landlord's daughter was a traveling salesperson who lived in the apartment next door. She said she often heard singing and sometimes smelled flowers, and that the place had once been a nursing home. The rent was cheap because of the unfinished bathroom and various broken pipes, yet the apartment had charm: ornate fireplace, hardwood floors, a large living room, and elegant light fixtures. Because the house appeared abandoned, antique dealers would break into the ground floor just to look around; we even joined them sometimes. It was fully furnished, with tiled fireplaces and parquet floors. Sheets covered the furniture, and in one room, there was evidence—clothing and food wrappers—that someone had squatted there in the past.

The haunting began with the sound of rocking. There were two rocking chairs in the hallway outside our door, but when we looked out, they were silent and motionless. Around midnight, we would hear footsteps in the attic above our bedroom, someone walking in a circle.

The attic door was unlocked, down the end of a dark hall. Behind it millions of pigeons had lived and died; they raised whole families and fought great battles over territory and love. There was a broken window from which they gained entry and the bodies of birds covered the floor.

There were so many odd noises that we stopped paying attention. One day a man knocked on the door asking for directions. When I looked down I saw his erection and slammed the door. I got my sister and a frying pan for a weapon, and we went looking for him. An elderly man on the street even joined the hunt, but we never found him.

The stalking started after my sister moved away; I was living alone and working at Firestone Steel, one of five women among two hundred men. I was nineteen and fresh from the wilds of Spencer County, just like Abe Lincoln, and I wore full makeup everywhere. I had graduated from a modeling school called Beautiful People, and as a result of my modeling education, I always, even in the steel plant, wore eye makeup, powder, and lipstick. A story appeared about me in the local newspaper about how I was a welder and a model. I was made a Kentucky Colonel, but turned down an invitation to the Kentucky Governor's mansion.

First, someone opened the transom above the door and left it standing open. The second time it happened, I secured the transom with a butter knife. The third time, I came home and there were cigarette butts in a heap outside the door like he had been waiting for me. I never spent the night there again. I moved and did not give anyone my address or phone number.

I never found out who my stalker was, but years later I heard that a Peeping Tom lived next door. Also there was a man at the plant, a stranger, who gave me an extravagant Valentine's Day present out of the blue. Years later, I met a woman who had lived in the landlord's daughter's apartment. She talked about how the apartment was so thick with roaches that they were beneath the wallpaper eating the glue. That's a sure sign of haunting, masses of uncontrollable vermin.

The Civil War soldier is buried in the loneliest part, although on Veterans Day he gets a flag. There has never been a sign of weeding or grave tending, all the regular marks of a surviving family. We gave him flowers and traced the carved letters of his name, and we wondered what he looked like and where his kin was, and since we knew when he died, we wondered how.

We placed flowers on all the bare graves, sometimes taking bouquets from others, making sure the neglected got something or making bouquets out of ditch lilies and daisies from the roadsides: gathering roses, the wild and thorny pink with tiny blossoms, and trumpet vines, finding a vase, or tin can covered in foil for beauty. Beauty and memory and fairness were our aims.

By the time my grandfather died, the other WWI vets were as feeble as he was. What a sight to see them lift a loaded coffin, play taps, and fire a twenty-one-gun salute. The flag folded in a triangle rests in my mother's bureau drawer.

Our neighbor from the trailer on the corner posed with a feather duster next to her onyx double headstone. She died shortly thereafter. Her double header reads "together in life, together in death," but he's still alive and has a girlfriend now. He owns too many acres, his parents' and his uncle's farms, to ever see them separated. He'll never leave his trailer on the corner that looks out over his acreage, won't sell the church next door the lot it wants for expansion although he's been a member since birth.

He likes to look out his trailer window and say, "This is God's country."

Here is the mounted oval portrait of Mrs. Parker, stuck in the nineteenth century and in the silver fenced-off plot. No one held the fancy fence against them. All the Parkers (Walter was our grade school principal with his three wives who all died of natural causes) are there. Plus it was a good place to keep captured dogs. I loved to play tag among the headstones; it made an excellent base.

And us, we are out of ground, and our graves meet the road.

Some neighbors went up to Chrisney to be buried by the golf course and water tower on a bare hill, and others to the county seat. One went to join his legs, amputated from diabetes, already buried. Some thought they were coming here, but the survivors had other plans. Some can only be found by a grave dowser with a tree branch. Something about the soil, the density of it, causes the branches to bend down.

There is Red's grave (upholsterer and neighbor whose father Elise was the grave mower with his powerful mules), Jake and Gertie (farmers) from the tarpaper house that was built on a sandstone boulder. Harold, from the corner (farmer and carpenter) who brought my father soup, lies a few yards over.

I never knew the rest of you.

Little lambs that mark children's graves, never knew you.

Husband and wife, who lie under the marble tower, never knew you.

George Reiz, the postmaster, my father's boss, never knew you.

McCoys, homesteaders who built our house and barn, never knew you.

I only knew the land beneath our feet and the alignment of planets over our heads.

My sister placed a brand new set of socket wrenches in my father's coffin. The coffin was not very plush: in fact, it was bottom of the line; my mother wanted to spend a thousand dollars more for a plumped-up one, but we talked her out of it because he had always said not to worry about the dead, it is the living who suffer. The burial policy and veteran's benefits gave us about five thousand to spend, just enough to cover the cost, including something for my uncle Harry who worked part time for the funeral home. My father said he didn't want any flowers, just a rose in a Coke bottle. But he did get flowers, some with angels that played music; he got baskets and plants, most still living.

My father didn't have a suit, so we buried him in Uncle Jim's old clothes and thought we better call Little Jimmy and warn him, so he wouldn't be shocked to see my dad laid out in his father's suit. We sent my father out into the cold darkness, wearing another man's clothes.

When I think of death, I tell myself that I'm going to where my father is, and if he's there, that's a good place to be. I'm going to the place where all have gone before me, and that's what makes me human.

Narrative of Abduction

He was relic hunting on the Wabash River bottoms, but only for items on the surface, because he had once taken a skull from an ancient grave and bad luck had followed until he returned it. He had a friend with him and they came across an open grave with an unusually long skeleton in it. Remembering his bad luck, they decided to fill in the grave. That's when they heard the bees buzzing; several hours later, they woke up.

Under hypnosis, he recalled being transported onto a spaceship. He divorced later (he told me that his wife didn't like for him to talk about the abduction), and his friend was institutionalized because he refused to believe that the whole thing had happened, even though the aliens had embedded a piece of metal in his scalp. MUFON (Mutual UFO Network) says it's one of the best cases they ever had, and this happened around the same time and place that a train had run backwards trying to get away from a bright light coming down the tracks.

In the 1970s, there were waves of reported unidentified flying objects. My sister saw a UFO land and disappear into the old gnarly oak in the pasture. The one I saw was a cylinder with a stovepipe sticking out, floating in the sky far away. Could have been a dream, not sure; for I once saw a toucan outside our kitchen window, and that must have been a dream. A poet told me that he saw a UFO that seemed at first glance to be a tumbling house.

Enough already, let's get in the river bottoms with the weird things.

In Lily Dale, at the Maplewood Hotel, a portrait of Lincoln and a tapestry hung, both done while in a trance. We went to the Inspiration Stump, a concrete tree stump in the woods, for messages. I had heard an account of a poet who went and the medium saw boxes all around her—and the poet was in the process of moving! One psychic sang all of her predictions. They weren't recognizable tunes, but little impromptu songs. The others (psychics) were freestyle, giving out impressions and visions. One saw my grandmothers holding up my arms like I was a prizefighter, and said that a ten-year-old spirit boy helps me teach young people. None of which I can disprove.

We went to the chapel for the laying on of hands. The organist played "Love Me Tender," and we sat on chairs in the sanctuary while they moved their hands, sometimes touching us and sometimes not, generating heat over our bodies. We met a mother with two little blond girls who had had pictures of their spirit guides drawn for one hundred dollars. The spirit guides were also blond and wearing the same outfits, and they had bright rainbows surrounding their heads, like the kind of halo you see in a old picture of Christ, only in pastels, not gold.

They did not allow photography. When Simon, a paranormal poet, tried to film three mediums washing a car, they froze until he put down the camera. We watched a video about how the town psychics owned their own houses, but the church owned the land. So if any psychic misbehaved, they would have to take their house and leave.

There were slate writings in the museum; the medium puts a piece of chalk or a pencil between two slates and somehow the spirits are able to write. The letters are backwards and almost like hieroglyphics. Maybe this is a transmission problem, like a bad connection, since they are writing from the other side. However, I can read them with a mirror even though my third eye is nearsighted.

My sister joined the army when she was eighteen years old and got shipped off to Alabama. In her barracks there was a red stain on the floor of the bathroom. It was the bloodstain of a girl who stabbed herself to death. Every time they removed the stain, it always came back. One night the women in her company decided to have a seance in order to contact the dead girl. During the seance, they panicked and stopped without closing the circle. After that night, my sister began to feel pressure on her chest. Over the next few months it gradually increased until finally it took the shape of an old man who called her a whore. He began to choke her, growing in strength. She transferred to Germany in order to get away from him, but he followed her. She went to a priest, was blessed and sprinkled with holy water, and that ended the haunting.

One evening, about a month after my father died, as I was reading, I noticed the lights flicker, so I told my husband that we needed to have them checked. The next night, the last dream I had before rising was of my father sitting at the kitchen table in his usual spot. I could tell that he felt good by his body language and expression. He might even have been smoking a pipe.

That morning, at the beginning of class, something rare occurred: the lights went out for a few seconds, and the room was completely dark. Then I knew for sure.

Elaine, the second oldest, had a dream in which he said it was o.k. for us to go shopping. Brother Kenneth had a visitation. Will he reveal it? Will Peggy, the youngest daughter? And why has he never come to my mother in a dream?

Thomas Edison spent the last years of his life trying to build a machine that would allow us to speak to and see the dead. But he died and so . . .

The students found hair that even the high school science teacher couldn't identify, although they didn't tell the teacher where they found it.

Here's a picture of the terrain. There are caves and springs and woods and a farmer's field nearby. This arrow, that's the place where the shape was seen. This arrow points to broken branches, right where it was spotted. A pile of dried grass, bent and heaped up, could be a nest.

A man wrote, "Makes high pitched screams, shot into the woods, each night it comes closer. No one believed us and slammed the door in our faces. Not there anymore, the cabin on the edge of woods, someone dismantled it and built a brick home."

This thing lives mostly in California, Ohio, and Indiana. One witness says it comes back every few years to throw rocks, and he can smell it coming. This one says he's going to bait and observe this winter. He makes references to having some experience but gives no details, and this hunter says people just want to make money off his story.

Shine a light at it and its eyes glow red. Shine a light at a bear's eyes, you get green. That's the difference.

The Shed

Directions: This is a very easy film to make as the hogs are predictable in their behavior and limited in range by the pen; however, they are deceased, and I took part in eating them, thus this is a most difficult film to make. Build a three-room shed out of wood with a tin roof and flathead nails. Plant thistles and pigweed. Dig a wallow and fill with water.

Narrative: The pig shed is gone and where it stood are green grasses. A neighbor bought half of the land and put up a stable of goats (says they are the main ingredient in pepperoni). I can remember our pigs without the aid of hypnosis or memory drugs. There's Pearl, the mama. Rusty with his reddish patches (my pig), and Dogfood (Peggy's pig).

Can you capture the sound of my hog call?

We stocked the wallow with tadpoles, who died despite our efforts.

Film us (four girls) in the wallow, deepening the hole.

Can you film us thinking "If we could only float a boat in here then we would truly have everything: water, mud, and navigation."

Shoot a close-up of nose rings and film us scraping our plates into a coffee can, turning dinner into hog slop. Can you film the ghost of Pearl? Pan out to the humans, on bicycles and foot, rooting in junkyards on the old Moore place, rooting in ravines full of abandoned cars.

I try to ride my pig but fall off. I pet my pig. Lay my head down on his rump. I am a small human, so small that my underpants come up to my armpits. Buster Weatherholt's dog, Old Blue, always sat down when I tried to ride him. I sat on his back, then he sat down on hind legs and I slid off.

We wanted machines or animals for transport: swings, merry-go-rounds, and maypoles for flying. We tried to ride everything our size, living or not. Ponies were too high up. We considered a wooden wagon with wooden wheels; we could take to the prairies in this, but we needed a team. I dreamed of so many treasures buried in the earth or of just bones, all the bones buried by time, nature, or natives. Given eternity, we could find marvelous bones.

Several people offer to help us with our monsters. What do you mean by help? I ask, not sure if they intended to offer moral support or to help us capture the creature. Although we read the sign that said, "Take only memories," we want to borrow our creature as proof of something bigger than ourselves and our big box stores, presidential funerals, and wars. This creature could cause all the books to be rewritten, all of science to pause and start over again. A harmless swatch of sweat or spit, the DNA is all we need, but we must get close enough to put a swab in its ear. We intend to give the monster back, not to murder it. Our trap? We need wire and steel, to build a cage to contain it, or we could live in the cage, in the thick of the deep woods protected by steel.

My sister made a spirit board and used a paper cup as a pointer. She asked the spirits to help her solve the local murder of a ten-year-old girl in Christmas Lake Village. She investigates from the living room of her house by the Green River in Kentucky, where many tragedies and mysteries have occurred. Despite all the supernatural help, she hasn't solved one mystery yet.

My roommate used a board to contact a spirit. When she asked his name, the pointer spelled out S-A-T-A-N.

We never swam in the Ohio River because everyone warned, "Look out for the undertow." I thought they meant the under-troll and envisioned a population of trolls who lived on the river bottom, whose purpose was to drown swimmers. I liked to read the story of Billy Goat Gruff, and I liked to think about it and about how Billy Goat Gruff crossed the bridge without getting eaten by the awful troll. That's why I won't swim there ever. It stinks. It's muddy, there's broken glass on the bottom, and it's only blue from a distance.

She had never seen anything like them before. They had very long bodies, pointy snouts, their teeth were made of baleen, but they were not paddlefish. Her husband kept catching them and bring-ing them home even though they didn't eat them. She brought some over—they were dead, dead as doorknobs. We all said we'd never seen anything like them before. They were very old fish, we decided. My mother made a stew for the dogs out of the very old fish with their long snouts of baleen.

A man bought a rundown funeral home. His family and friends were puzzled because it was a money pit. After a year or so of pouring money into the place, he committed suicide—an overdose of pills. He left precise instructions for his burial, the clothes, the service. He videotaped his suicide, saying not to blame his therapist because he had hidden his death wish so well and buying the funeral home was a part of his plan to control his own death and memorial service.

I got very upset at the thought that I could be a fictional character in the dream of a dog, but I feel pain and thus think I'm real.

A poet said that her brother, a member of the fire department's bomb squad, posed for a formal portrait of his company. In the photo he is surrounded by a halo, but no one else is. At a wedding, the same thing happened: out of all of the members of the wedding party, even the bride, only he is surrounded by light. A short time later, at the World Trade Center, his company went into one of the towers. He returned to the truck to fetch some equipment, just before the building collapsed. He was the only one of his company who survived.

A teenager was driving home through the woods when he saw a very tall mechanical creature in the rearview mirror.

At Niederstein's, a German restaurant in Middle Village, is a 150-year-old inn built around the cemetery trade. Trouble with lights? I asked the waiter. He hesitated and admitted yes, there were problems with the lights caused by the ghost of the owner's mother who had lived in an apartment upstairs and died recently.

A couple saw a pterodactyl in Kentucky, with red skin, knob on the nose, pointed head, and a twenty-foot wingspan. This was in 2005.

PART II
THE ROBERT INVESTIGATIONS

Librarium

The Chapel of the Chimes

I

The furnace was dead that day, so no smoke or ash hung in the sky. By mistake I had taken a wrong turn and ended up at the crematorium, a nineteenth-century building composed of four stories of ash and metal, fountains and spiral staircases. Each wing was named after a flower. The shelves were eighteen feet high and filled with urns, some larger and more elaborate than others. Some were shaped like loving cups with handles, and some had been removed from the shelves leaving empty spaces for rent. Later on, I was shown the correct building, a columbarium, where book-shaped urns sat on enormous bookshelves. Some books were longer and wider than others, some fancier, and the blank spots? I could be endowed and hold this space until the end of time. This is a very good resting place for a poet. See this naked spine, and my name in print. Brenda Gayle Coultas 1958–20__? I plan to someday sneak in and alphabetize all the ashes.

II

Beyond the Librarium was a cemetery that opened in 1863. There was a man sitting in a car; he smiled at me, so I gave him a dirty look. I could have be raped out there in the quiet, open space; a couple of lovers were lying on the green below—they couldn't see me up on the hill. All the men I saw on the way in were gray, and I saw only one woman, also gray, smoking furiously and dressed in a business suit.

I tried to stay in sight of the public, on the road, although there was little traffic. A delivery truck came and dropped something off at the stonemason's house. Maybe there were eyes there? This is not Alphabet City, the East Village, or New York City, I told myself. This is not a place I know, and I became angry at my friend Robert for not coming with me, although I hadn't asked him and had felt that I could take care of myself.

Meanwhile, he came looking because he had an urgent feeling about my safety. In the Librarium, he called out my name in case I was in one of the chapels or looking at the old bibles on display. He met a man who asked him if he were yelling "Annabella" in a weird voice. The man, who was wearing white shoes and a shiny dark suit, said that it might be disturbing to other visitors. Robert said, "No, I was yelling, 'Brenda,'" and he demonstrated. Then, out of the corner of his eye, Robert saw something move, so he turned his head, nothing there. When he turned back around the man had vanished. Later, he realized that the shoes were from the disco era.

III

A day later, we returned to drive around further. There were entire sections marked "unendowed." The unendowed were overrun with trash and brush. We got out of the car and poked around at the dirty graves, digging through brush for the names and dates. Later on we walked up the hill to visit the endowed; although all trimmed, they were also neglected.

A week later, Robert returned alone. There were many people on the grounds. He drove by a couple, a man and woman dressed in black, who yelled an insult at him. Robert said, "What's your problem, mister?" The woman walked up and said, "His problem is people like you, that's what's wrong with him." Robert drove away and when he looked back, they were butting their heads together. The End.

ADDENDUM I: It turned out that the man in the disco shoes was not a phantom, devil, alien, hologram, astral projection, or figment of the imagination. A few weeks later, Robert saw him again. This time he witnessed the man in the cemetery, being handcuffed by the police. The man was wearing a shirt from the seventies, with long collar points that reached down to his breastbone.

ADDENDUM II: I asked Robert if he would return with his psychic friend. They planned to go on a Saturday, but the friend had a dream in which someone was snapping their fingers, so she fell deeply asleep. Later in the week, she began seeing tails, hairless slithering tails, and Robert had seen one too.

ADDENDUM III: They met and she, the psychic friend, wore a special outfit, something Eastern, for protection. About one block before the crematorium, she heard a trumpet, but Robert did not. She began to speak in voices and dance in circles. An elderly woman came out and asked if they had heard the trumpet too. She said she knew what was going on but wouldn't tell them. Instead she pointed to a house with the front blind partly drawn; inside was an old man staring out. She told them that he heard voices, yet she would not elaborate.

Psychic friend fell into a deep sleep, and Robert held her. This lasted for an hour. He told himself that he was stronger than any demons. When she awoke, she said she wouldn't tell him anything, for his own protection. She only said that he needed to be strong. He has seen her since, but she, the psychic friend, will not say what it was that she experienced.

ADDENDUM IV: The psychic friend explained that the old woman was a daylight person, which is a living person who has become lost or passed into a portal. The portal is analogous to a clear shower curtain; you walk through it and everything looks the same, but actually you are in a different dimension. It may only be a few feet wide, so you might not be able to find it again.

She said there is no evil, only negativity; however, the portal on the crematorium lawn should not be open. In regard to her behavior, the odd dancing and trance, she reported that spirits who had died by their own actions, accidentally or intentionally, were standing in front of her face, explaining their regrets and intentions. During this time, she, the psychic friend, experienced a continuous orgasm, which allowed her to withstand the intense negative energies.

A woman at a yard sale told Robert this story about spending the night there. She was out for a walk when she heard a woman and man arguing. She could not locate the voices, but the argument was growing heated. She looked for them among the crypts. One voice said "It's all your fault." She heard them call each other Gladys and Fred. She resumed walking and she saw a family gathered around a headstone, and the names Gladys and Fred were inscribed on it.

At closing time, the guard cleared everyone out and a dog ran in. Worried that it was lost, she went after it, got locked in, and spent the night inside the cab of a tractor on the grounds. She kept hearing a crackling noise, and every time she tried to leave the cab, she felt sick. The dog would bark but when she let him out, he wanted right back in. Afterwards, for a year, she only related to animals, and she was afraid to go out at night.

A Narrative of a Haunting at the Winchester House

Robert wanted you to hear this story about a woman who visited a famous haunted mansion in what was once an orchard, but now is surrounded by malls, including a haunted Toys "Я" Us. He hardly knows her; she is someone from work. He doesn't know her history or her reason for telling this story. When she found out where we'd been, she said, "I never want to go through that hell again." But she is not the subject of the haunting, she is a witness.

The house belonged to the widow of the Winchester rifle fortune. After the deaths of her husband and baby daughter, Mrs. Winchester began consulting a medium who told her that she was being haunted by the ghosts of people who were killed by Winchester rifles. In order to keep a step ahead of the ghosts that pursued her, Mrs. Winchester communicated with spirit guides nightly, and they created new floor plans in the seance room. She built 160 rooms, along with fake stairs and doors designed to throw the angry spirits off her trail.

The woman who told us the story described how she and two other women took the tour of the house on a slow day, and they fell behind the group. One of the three dared to lie down on Mrs. Winchester's deathbed. It was not the original deathbed because after Mrs. Winchester's death, the estate was broke, so they sold the furniture. However, the bed was one that matched the nineteenth-century decor as closely as possible and was most likely placed in the original spot where Mrs. Winchester had died in her sleep. The subject lay down on Mrs. Winchester's bed and the other two women rejoined the tour.

At first, the subject felt warm, and very relaxed; then she began to feel sick, and she was held down on the mattress by an unseen force. When she was able to get out of the bed, she dragged herself to the nearest chair. A woman wearing a nurse's cap and an apron appeared, pushed her out into the hallway, and said, "You've done enough, go on." Her friends thought that she was still with them on the tour, and at the end, they realized that it's not their friend, but someone who looked like her from a distance. They asked the tour guide to search for her because she could have wandered off into any of the 160 rooms.

They found their missing friend in a section of the house that was severely damaged in the San Francisco quake. There were no furnishings, no repairs were ever made. It was raw space. During the quake, Mrs. Winchester was trapped in a nearby bedroom for a day. Near that room, they found the subject standing in a corner, wet. Her hair, which had been permed and on top of her head, was straight as a board and covered her face. The subject said that someone had been spitting or blowing in her hair. She was drenched in a liquid, but it was not sweat.

For the next thirteen days all three women were sick with a flu-like illness, and everyone that they told their tale to also became sick for thirteen days, a number Mrs. Winchester had been obsessed with.

A Reflection on a Paranormal Encounter

Robert theorizes that the Winchester House is haunted but not in the way that we thought. During our visit, he believes that a spirit attached itself to him, enabling and influencing meetings and events in his life. Robert has become a confessional, not for sinners, but for people who have witnessed unusual phenomena. A lawyer at an office where he delivers mail told him a story about an encounter that happened a week before, in what she terms "a safe neighborhood." She was walking and someone dressed in an odd costume ran by her very fast. She thought "this is a safe place," so she was not too concerned. She continued walking and she heard a loud noise, a voice? There was something standing in the shadow of a tree, and she had the clarity of mind as a lawyer to observe and memorize the details. In the shadow was a creature with a man's face. He looked Arabic and very old, and the rest of his body was blue. At first, she thought it was someone wearing a Halloween costume, except that the creature had haunches. He was urgently speaking to her in some sort of pig Latin, and in his hands he held a blue light, which he extended toward her. As she leaned in to hear better, a group of her friends approached, calling out her name, and he sprinted away.

There could be a witness. One friend asked her whom she was talking to. She has told only Robert this story, and she has given him permission to share it with me, an unlicensed poetic investigator. Since then, he has returned to her office to deliver packages, but he hasn't seen her. When he asked if the witness was on vacation or ill, the coworker implied that she was both. She did return to work and only referred to it as something that happened for which she has no explanation.

Later he heard a woman call into a radio show and describe a similar event. In fact, he thought it was the same person. When Robert did see her again, she had quit her job and planned to work in an art gallery. Her style of dress had changed, too. She no longer wore corporate suits. Instead she wore flowing types of dresses and had loosened her long hair.

Update, February 23, 2005. During the rains in Los Angeles this week, many residents report that a creature larger than a mountain lion and resembling a gargoyle had been sighted.

Robert told me this story, but he can't remember if he overheard or dreamed it. Every day for a month a butcher knife, the old-fashioned kind, appeared stuck into a tree in the same position. At first, the neighbors removed the knife so that neighborhood kids wouldn't play with it, but in the morning another knife would appear. There was an oily substance on the blades and there were random letters carved into the handles. At the end of the month, the knives stopped appearing. That weekend four neighbors were stabbed to death. A homicide detective working the case heard the story. He thought there might be a clue in the weird letters on the handles, so he collected the knives and found that the letters made up the names of the four victims.

Robert, whom I've known for thirty years, is my co-investigator. He is Irish, Blackfoot, and a vegan. His father comes from the wilds of Kentucky and was a shell-shocked WWII veteran; his mother was an Irish war bride who always regretted moving to the United States. He had three sisters; one, Bessie Ann, died at eight months old in Ireland. Throughout his life, Bessie Ann has visited him. When he was a child, he would see his mother in his room, chasing away a gray shape and then covering him up with a blanket. One sister is psychic as the result of an unborn twin who attached itself to her uterus. His father worked at Fall City beer plant, sang along at a piano bar called Peg's, and rode a bike. His mother dyed her hair with shoe polish and shook her fist at her husband and always said, "I'm gonna kill him."

There was evidence of paranormal activity during his childhood. When his father was laid off, he would regularly find thirty-five cents, the admission price to the local movie theater, on the ground. He even heard the clinking of the coins as they fell from the sky.

Robert's shoes are paint-splattered. He found his calling as a painter in midlife. He is nonjudgmental and accepts the absurd but will not tolerate injustice. As a result, he has been in several fistfights. Women like to confess the bizarre, the taboo, or come on to him. Once a woman in a convenience store handed him a condom and said, "Here's my calling card." He wears his shirts open a button or two lower than most men.

After our Winchester House visit, he met two women: one is a healer he calls the Angel Lady, and the other is called

Annabella, also referred to as psychic friend in this investigation. The two women are friends and share visions and impressions. Recently, both had similar nightmares that led them to travel together to Brazil for encounters with flying objects. When Robert asked, "Do you mean UFOs?" the Angel Lady replied, "No, IFOs, they are Identified Flying Objects." During the Angel Lady's dream, she wakes up in a small mansion, opens a door to a garden, and sees little lights blinking in code. As she travels downhill, the setting changes into a train station in a jungle. People wearing red gowns point and lights surround her for her protection. The Angel Lady then skips a part, which is not to be revealed even to Robert. In Annabella's dream the lights are movie screens, but it's the same train station and lights, plus a vision of creatures descending from clouds and feeding her answers.

He was introduced to the Angel Lady by Annabella because he was feeling poorly. He is not allowed to know her real name, but because of her natural glow and healing powers, he named her the Angel Lady. She provided him with a magic word for spiritual protection and healing.

One day he ran into the Angel Lady at a health food store and she said, "Watch for colors." He thought she meant the paint splatters on his clothes. That day he saw a flash of black, and it was a dog that had jumped out of a window and landed in the bushes. If he hadn't seen it, the owners wouldn't have found the dog. A woman in red talking on a cell phone was almost run over by a truck. Robert pushed her out of the way. A kid in blue running ahead of his mother. Robert caught him before he ran into traffic.

The Angel Lady predicted an event in which an unusual thought would prevent a brutal act. A week later there was an incident involving a prowler with a knife. Robert knocked the prowler down and held a shovel to the prowler's throat. At that moment, as he stood above the prowler, about to plunge the blade into the man's throat, he had an odd thought about his recent UFO sighting, of a formation of red lights flying over Oakland. This thought gave him a moment to think about the consequences, and he let the prowler go.

A Series of Dreams About a Loved One

Bob the Cat died and Robert was grieving the loss of "this small creature." The cat was quite old and had suffered from cancer greatly in his last month. Robert cremated him and stores Bob's ashes in a sandwich baggie. Thus began a series of dreams about Bob the Cat. In the first one, Robert dreamed of Bob dressed as a detective, and they were ascending a staircase with a handrail made of hands with manicured nails. Robert says, "What a cliché!" and one of the hands reaches out and scratches him. Bob looks at him and says "This is really gonna hurt," and a long red cape grows from the back of Robert's neck. He turns into a beast, and as they fly down the stairs, he views portraits of family members, circa 1800s, which he is supposed to remember, but can't. The portraits turn into light.

Later on, as Bob leads him through this netherworld, Robert encounters Raylette the Radio Ray Girl, a character that he invented in high school. Since she is from another planet, she believes that Robert is a god, not realizing that he is merely human. Raylette asks him, "Are you the haunted one?" On Robert and Bob's bodies are tattoos that read: "Rumors of sleep, rumors of adrenaline" and "This is black eye for pretty."

The second dream takes place in a long warehouse and there's a redheaded kid in a striped T-shirt and blue jeans. Robert sees something light falling down: it is an angel that has been harpooned. As the angel falls, it lands on the redheaded kid, pinning them both to a chair. Bob plucks out a feather for a quill and writes in a book. When Robert tries to look over his shoulder, Bob says, "No, not yet." The dreams that follow involve the book, and every time Robert tries to read it or look over Bob's shoulder, something violently thwarts him.

During the course of this investigation, Robert called me regularly to report on anomalies in his neighborhood.

Odd events continued at the Librarium. I asked Robert to return and pick up any pamphlets about the history of the cemetery and crematorium. When he went to the cemetery to ask for information, an employee began talking to him about funeral arrangements she had made for his family. When he tells her that she is mistaken about his identity, she begins to cry. It turns out that she believed Robert to be her long-lost cousin, Alejandro, who had just lost his entire family in an automobile accident.

Robert called to report two seemingly related events in his neighborhood: the water in the creek caught fire, and that two men heard a Godzilla-like roar come from a culvert that feeds the creek; within minutes they were in the culvert with flashlights, but found nothing.

About a month later, Robert was walking near the creek when he came across a couple from the neighborhood. Robert remarked on how wonderful it was to be spending the longest day of the year in the park. The woman said, "Yes, it really is the longest." They began discussing the creek and how Robert and some other neighbors had stopped people from dumping paint and toxic waste into the water. When Robert mentioned the water catching fire, they told him their story.

On that longest day, they were having a picnic on the bridge when they heard a moaning coming from underneath. The man went down to look and saw nothing, so he came back up. At that point, the woman was on the bank when they saw flames, the size of a small table, floating rapidly down the stream. And for about one second, she saw the outline of a human being drowning in the flames.

Robert followed up on the story by asking a science librarian how the creek could catch fire, and how the animal sound could possibly be related. The librarian said the sound could have been feral cats; they often make a loud sound for their own protection. Also, in the summer the water runs slower and a patch of oil could ignite. As for the human outline in the flames, it was most likely a shadow. Then he added that once he saw the air catch fire. He was about thirty feet away and he saw a flame suddenly appear in the air; it even looked as if it were trying to take on a shape. As a science-minded observer, he looked for a natural explanation. He even returned to the spot the next day to see if he could solve the mystery of the freestanding flame in the air. He concluded that there was no explanation.

PART III
SECONDHAND STORIES

THE FOURTH OF JULY

On the Fourth of July, a poet told me this story. Dave runs his family's 250-year-old bar in the French Quarter of New Orleans. The haunting became active when he changed it from a biker bar and hotel into a single-family dwelling and a gathering place for artists and poets. The upstairs apartment has about ten rooms with twenty-foot ceilings and shuttered windows. He theorizes that the spirits come from the emotions of the previous tenants who were lonely or battling personal demons in the old single-room apartments.

Some of the spirits are charming. For example, when I visited the bar, the spot near the ceiling, where one familiar spirit sometimes appears, was pointed out; at first glance, this ghost looks like a haze of cigarette smoke hanging in the air, but as one keeps looking, a woman dressed in white becomes clear.

However, the subject of this story is a malignant spirit. After they moved in, his wife began feeling someone scratch her as she walked up the stairs. The scratching increased in intensity and regularity until one day it drew blood, and the entity began sitting in a corner of their bedroom at night and was entering their dreams. Dave asked a friend, a hoodoo practitioner, how to vanquish the spirit. The friend warned him not to give in to the entity's manipulations. He warned, "You have to think of them as pests," and he told Dave to call upon his ancestors and ask them to walk through the space and help him claim it. He did, but things got worse. He began to battle the entity in his dreams. One night he awoke and knew that it was in the bar, and he went down for the confrontation. At first he saw a jester (a human spirit), and

it ran behind the bar and through a wall. He was relieved, think-
ing that was easy. Then he saw another one farther back, by the
bathrooms. It was huge and made of garbage, like something you
see next to an incinerator. This was not human, he said, this was
the one that has been tormenting him. Dave told him that only
one of them could stay and it was going to be him. Dave realized
his enemy's weakness: it could not stand the thought of *not exist-
ing*. It would feed off of anything and do anything in order to be.
He held his ground even though the entity threatened to harm
the people Dave loved. The spirit struggled, threatened, and then
fled through the wall. He has not seen it since.

The following Fourth of July, Dave told me this. Because of Hurricane Katrina, he, his pregnant wife, and his young daughter moved to Natchez to stay with relatives. Unsure of how long they would have to stay after the storm, they rented a house about a mile from his wife's aunt and uncle. Dave and his family, plus his mother-in-law, moved in. On the first night, Dave fell asleep holding hands with his wife and daughter, grateful that he had his family with him, safe for the moment. In the middle of the night he awoke and saw a ghost of a man dressed in pants, shirt and tie, sixties or seventies style, walking up the stairs to their bedroom.

Even though the ghost was fully materialized, Dave knew that this was not a living person, and suspects that the ghost enacted this ritual every night because it recalled his daily return home during his mortal life. When the ghost realized that Dave could see him, he was shocked. In his mind, Dave told the ghost that he must leave, that he (Dave) had his own problems, serious ones. The ghost became very sad; the intensity of the sadness akin to Dave's despair.

As the ghost left, Dave pleaded with him to come back, saying that they could work something out. Dave followed him out the door to a grassy patch across the driveway. There was a shimmering oval in the grass; floating within the oval was a knife. The ghost walked into the oval and was slowly absorbed.

The next day, Dave was in his car drinking coffee, listening to the radio for news from New Orleans. He met his new neighbor, an older lady, who told him that the house he was renting had been empty for years. She recalled the former occupants as the perfect family: a doctor, his wife and daughter, nothing unusual about them except for the doctor, whom she described as having an aura of sadness surrounding him.

Later, Dave found out that there had been a shooting in the house and the doctor had been badly hurt. He did, however, survive. The shooting was ruled a self-inflicted accident. There were rumors that his daughter had had a drug problem and that she or her mother had shot him. But what role did the shining weapon play? What message did the doctor wish to communicate?

My Sister's Story

"Have you seen anything of a tale of two cities?" Mr. Shirrer said.
—Written on the flyleaf of *The Handbook of Composition*, by my grandmother.

I asked my sister to tell me a story. She said, "Our grandmother was very ill and lying in bed worrying about who would raise her children when her mother appeared to her in a vision and said, 'Don't worry Nannie, it will be all right.' After that, she stopped worrying and recovered."

After many years, my sister quit the carnival and began working in a factory. I asked her to tell me a story, and she told me about a retired stripper who passes out candy and cheer during her factory shift and who dances, for old time's sake, at the dive down the street. One night some old guy in the club said, "Thanks, I needed that."

Later in the week, she called with two stories. She said a man walked into a bar and ordered a drink. He was so obnoxious that the bartender put pickle juice in his drink and he never noticed. In fact, he ordered another one and every time he went to the bathroom, the bartender added more pickle juice. When he didn't show up for work the next day, his friends broke into his house to check on him, but everything looked fine. There were no signs of a struggle or robbery. They looked in the bedroom and there was a lump under the covers. They pulled the covers back and found a large dill pickle. They said, "Well, he always wanted to be a big dill."

The other story? For the first time in twenty years she was living without an alcoholic in her house; she had to get used to the quiet.

The telephone business was troubling. She was getting divorced, so her emotions were running high. An angry male ghost might have been drawn to a troubled female? She was living alone in a fifty-year-old farmhouse on the west side of town, and she had not yet had her daughter.

She stepped outside to wait for her friend to pick her up, but the friend was late so she went back in. She heard the sound a phone makes when a receiver is off the hook. It was. Which was odd, for she clearly remembered hanging the phone up properly before she went outside. She put it back on and the friend called and said, "Why are you playing games with me? I know it was you because I hear the same background music." During this time, her family's police dog never stirred or barked.

Later on that night, she was awakened by the sound of cats fighting in the backyard. She got up to check because she had an outdoor cat. She looked outside, no cats. She returned to bed, and as she was about to fall asleep, something woke her. Standing at the foot of her bed was the ghost of a man in a plaid shirt and blue jeans with his hands on his hips. He was headless and there for less than a minute. She thought she might have been dreaming but her socks were wet and grass-stained.

This was not the first encounter. When she was a little girl, her family moved into a farmhouse in the country, and they gave her an upstairs bedroom. In the middle of the night, she woke up and screamed. Later in this same house, her father went out of town; she and her mother were in bed. They heard a crashing sound, her mother got out of bed to see what it was. In the hallway a picture had crashed to the floor. There were three pictures hanging in the hallway. As they stood there, the second one crashed, then the third one.

I asked my cousin for some ghost stories, so he took me to a haunted jailhouse. A law firm now owns it, and there is only one remaining cell, which has been preserved. It's a four-story nineteenth-century building with a stone facade and turrets. Underneath is a tunnel that connects the jail to the courthouse across the street. Some people have seen apparitions in the basement by the tunnel doors. At the rear of the jail is a view of the courthouse with a statue of Liberty with her face turned away, which the lawyer found tragic because this was the last sight of the free world the prisoners saw. Although I took many digital pictures, none of them contained orbs or ectoplasm. I felt no creepiness, not even when I lay down on a steel bunk in the jail cell.

The odd thing was, my cousin, a master of tales, could not remember any ghost stories and remembered only one UFO encounter, near the Yankeetown river bottoms. There was a ball of light, which he and another cousin followed in their car, until it sank into the river and which made my other cousin cry.

My brother knows everything that happens in the county because he has an outdoor job that begins before dawn. He says the meth houses are the ones that have the lights on all night because anything you start on meth you keep doing for days until you crash, whether it's sex or cleaning. One guy took his TV apart and could never put it back together. Some people get "meth-bugs," which is when the chemicals in the meth start to seep out of the skin, making the meth-head scratch and claw open her or his skin. He even knew a guy who froze his balls off. The guy went out with some friends to steal anhydrous ammonia, a frozen gas the local farmers use for fertilizer and a major ingredient in meth. It's so malleable you can put it into any kind of container, so he put some into a paper cup, sat it between his legs, and drove off. The anhydrous ammonia spilled onto his balls and froze them off, and his friends kicked him out of the truck as they drove by the emergency room.

I did not find many ghost tales, but I did find crystal meth labs growing in the cornfields. Also, I found out that some members of the county road crew are swingers. I heard of one farmer who wife-swaps.

My friend, a poet, sent me two Polaroids taken less than a minute apart. The setting is an Adirondack campground in the summer and the subject is a group of eight campers holding hands and dancing in a circle. In the first photograph, the four figures in the front are clear, and if one looks closer, the other four dancers on the far side of the photo are visible.

In the second photo, taken less than a minute later, there is a white mist over the bottom half, and toward the upper right, there is a greenish light and hint of the dancers underneath the mist; however, they appear to have sprouted wings on their backs. To the left, a wispy group of angels led by a woman in white walk out of the frame.

He said the camp was very old, and many of the same families return each summer, and if he were a ghost, it is where he would want to be.

There is another event: his best friend died, and a year later, he traveled with her husband to the mountain town where she had always wanted to live, to a poetry summer camp. At the end of the week, all the poets gathered for a reading. My friend wanted to create a group collaboration and, thinking about how people love to hear their names called, he passed out cards, which on one side read "a word or words," and the other side read "name." The poets were instructed to write down whatever they wanted. After collecting the cards, he went through the stack at random, writing down the names and words in order to create a long poem that captured the essence of that week.

As he was composing the poem, midway through he came across a card on which someone had written in blue pencil, "Remember." There was a gap between the "r" and "e" and other letters were faint but readable. Before he turned the card over to read the name, he knew what it would say. The card read "Mara," the name of his late best friend.

This poet lives in an actively haunted farmhouse. The first time, she saw him full on. She described him as appearing to be in his fifties, gaunt, wearing a hat and matching tan pants and shirt. He was looking past her. Instantly, she knew that he was the one who had built the tongue-in-groove woodwork and the bookshelves. She saw him again about a dozen times, but never as full or straight on, mostly out of the corner of her eye.

Her two dogs also noticed the ghosts. The puppy yapped and growled at invisible presences, whereas the older dog, due to his experience and wisdom, learned to ignore the spirits that co-inhabited the house.

One weekend her parents were visiting, and she heard them downstairs watching TV and talking, so she went down to meet them but when she got close, all went quiet. The room was empty. Her parents were upstairs in bed, asleep.

One night she had some friends over, including one who had some psychic ability. They decided to have a seance in order to communicate with the house. Her friend asked the spirits to make their presence known; however, she was called away from the party by a family matter, and left the house without closing the seance, which is akin to leaving a psychic door open.

That night, two of the guests slept side by side, and each experienced the sensation of someone blowing on their eyelashes. But when they opened their eyes, there was no one there. The one detail that confirmed this phenomenon was this: both reported that the ghostly breath smelled like peanut butter. That same night, in her bedroom, the poet got chills and felt someone stroking her arm hair for about ten minutes. Later, she burned sage throughout the house. That quieted the activity down.

She theorizes that the house resists change by creating distractions for the owners. The previous owners, who had planned to replace the flooring, sold the house because they were divorcing. She recently sold the house because she has reunited with her ex-husband and is moving in with him, and the plans she had the architect draw up for remodeling will never be used. Another detail supports her theory: when the house came on the market, the realtor found a poem about the weather, written on a piece of wood and dated 1906, in the barn. The realtor returned it, saying the house wanted it back.

A Perception

This poet said that perhaps her ghost story was too boring, that nothing really happened, and that that small nothing was a perception or feeling, not an event.

Her boyfriend had an apartment in an art deco building in Minneapolis that was always dark. As soon as she got up in the mornings, she would open all the curtains and turn on the lights. Still, it remained dark. One day she was alone, listening to music and writing, when she felt like someone was watching her. When she went to adjust the stereo, she felt someone blowing on the hairs of her neck. When she told her boyfriend, he said, " I know. The apartment is haunted."

There was a roommate, a new age massage therapist, who once went over the apartment with a pendulum and found the energy completely negative. After our talk, she e-mailed to say that her boyfriend sometimes saw shapes appear on the apartment walls.

The Orange Dress

A poet told me this tale over a glass of wine on a rainy day. She is in her mid-to-late twenties, and this occurred when she had just graduated college. She had applied for only one job for the fall, and moved back home to save money, thinking she would be moving to Europe soon. The director had even flown in to interview her, which made her think she would surely be offered the position. But the offer didn't happen, and she was stuck at home while her other friends went off to begin their careers.

She had begun smoking but didn't want her family to know, so she would go out on the roof. In the attic her stepfather had stored his late wife's clothing in a cardboard wardrobe. One day, the poet decided to try on one of the dresses. The wardrobe was heavy and the opening was about chest-high, so the clothes could not fall out; they had to be pulled out by hand. She tried on an orange dress, and returned it very carefully to the wardrobe, so no one could tell that any of the clothing had been disturbed. She went out on the roof to smoke, and walked out onto the ledge thinking about her prospects for a career and of the highlight of her short life, which was winning a scholarship to Italy in high school, and thinking that that was enough, that it was downhill from then on, and that the prospects of creating a life as a poet were quite dim.

As she stood on the ledge of the roof, smoking and reviewing her life, she heard a loud noise, from the inside downstairs. Although she was alone in the house, she dismissed it, and then another thud, which sounded closer, got her attention. She stepped back from the ledge, and went into the attic. There was the orange dress that she had so carefully packed back into the wardrobe, not rumpled or in a heap, but laid out smoothly on the floor as if on a bed waiting for the owner to wear it. The poet remembered photos of her stepfather's late wife, and that she was always smiling, that she had been happy when she had worn these clothes, whereas the poet had tried on the dress in defiance, rebellion. She had never met the late wife and the late wife had never lived in the house and yet . . .

Before this poet told me his story, he talked about consensus reality, about what we as a society agree is real, and his feeling was that there are other realities, which sometimes cross over into ours. He had given the idea a lot of thought. On his bookshelves were many texts on ghosts and the supernatural. At the time the event he was describing occurred, he was a teenager living in a rented house in the South, with his father, stepmother, and her mother. His sister had moved out, and he had withdrawn emotionally from his family. He kept to himself, and frequently experimented with drugs.

It was the last year of his father's life. He had cancer and was bedridden: the only thing he could do was walk from the bathroom to the bedroom over and over. Shortly after his father died, the son saw him walking to the bathroom. The young poet told no one.

One day he came downstairs to the kitchen and heard his stepmother talking to a man in her bedroom. He couldn't make out the words but he could hear two voices.

He looked out the window for his stepbrother's car, and his stepmother's mother standing nearby said, "You're looking for Randy's car, aren't you? He isn't here. Whose voice is that? Sounds familiar? Haven't you seen your father?"

They opened the door and the stepmom was asleep in bed.

The father's ghost continued to make regular trips to the bathroom. My friend described the apparition as a film loop that plays over and over. His father never looked at or acknowledged any of his family members or varied his path to the bathroom. The poet's sister tried to get their father's attention by deliberately walking into his ghost, but that failed. The conversation in the bedroom baffled my friend. He wondered if the fact that his father was able to converse with his wife in her sleep meant that the ghost was aware of his own death?

Soon the poet and the rest of his family moved into an apartment building. One day, while visiting a friend, the friend's mother said that she knew the people who had moved into the old house. She asked my friend for a description of his dad. Then she said, "You know, he's still there." This shocked my friend who had believed that once the family left, his father would, too.

PART IV
SPIRIT TOLD ME

Mi Squaw Helen,

Heap glad to write on the scratch sheet to you and say with smiles of the Great Spirit whose folds wrap you around with tender mercies. Do I come unto you to bring strength home of spirit father much big room there for pale faces, red faces all kinds—to White Eagle for me been in upper hunting ground long time   Indian left Squam up I lived on earth before the rulership of chiefs was superseded by a republican form of government my people believed in justice, morality and love the great spirit was to them a loving father so me glad you here you here and say when corn much go thing is brighter for you—much wampum have you tender heart

White Eagle

My Dear,

Its lovely to linger near the scenes of earth to be near to hear what you have to say, to see what you do. What dreams I had of your future I thought to see you one of the noblest and best and there was no gift of worldly honor which I did not crave for you. No height which I did not think possible for you to reach so in many walls. You have attained to all I could desire for you are good. And true develop your rare gift of mediumship and someday you shall blossom forth and help humanity with that gift. I have much to write so hope for a chance to do so.

Mother

I took the first from a photo album of Lily Dale Psychic Camp postcards taped inside a notebook, and the second one from a journal in a black binder.

I could see the trajectory of her illness over a twenty-year span. The earliest notebook, circa 1945, had none of her writing, just transcriptions from clairvoyant cards. When I touched them, it was like holding ectoplasm; disembodied heads, bluish, ethereal, slanted writing. Her journals contained descriptions of objects shown to her in visions that she had recorded in precise detail: a hollow cross tossed into a chimney, a sword in the air, a sphinx floating above her mother's head. She pasted in messages channeled during spirit readings at churches.

1. Do you know someone that is pregnant?
It will be all right it will be something that you will hear about it will be alright.
2. Do you know someone out of body with a "lung infection"—gentleman very thin. O.K. now, not so old.
3. Do some praying—boys out in Switzerland T.B.—children. About one month after praying you will know.
4. You are having a problem at home. You cannot do much with a bull. You cannot catch it. He's sorry after but the damage is done. Upset mother no end. Meaning well but has undone every bit of good he's done. (plastic bag over head)
5. "escape"—away; Both can do with a long rest. Always under your feet.
6. prayers
7. Indian force holds "this" in check, very strong Indian force. "Karate" stops him suddenly (cuts him off).

Inside one of the journals, I found a postcard, of great value, from John Steinbeck. "Thank you Miss Cason for your letter. Sorry I haven't got time to respond to your letter, I have important things (for me anyway), John Steinbeck."

He had crossed out the Sag Harbor address; the typewriter had dropped some of the letters. I found a draft of her letter, thanking him for writing *Travels with Charley*. The other twenty volumes of her journal were filled with endless lists for self-improvement. She was overweight and homely; she inked comic books for a living of sorts, and her journals contain drawings of lusciously thin comic book women.

After her death, the journals were sold at auction for thirty dollars and then given to me, this poet.

POSTSCRIPT: The postcard has gone missing.

I own a plot for couples in a lonely cemetery and although it is a final resting place some people go there to party and do donuts in the driveway. I know of a cemetery where a man hangs out in his wife's crypt. He has a TV, blanket, and lawn chair and greets visitors as they walk by. A lonely man in a lively cemetery. By Bernadette's there is an unmarked cemetery in the cow pasture and inside a grove of rose bushes and cedars lie the trampled headstones of the town's mothers and fathers.

Across the street from our apartment, The Marble Cemetery, surrounded by a school, bars, and apartments, is home to a lot of notables. The crypt, with a Mayan glyph overhead, houses John L. Stephens, author of *Incidents of Travel in the Yucatán*. President Madison (or was it Monroe?) was once interred there.

A couple buried pets in their family cemetery. On a hill overlooking their house in the shadow of a mountain, he pointed to a headstone carving of a weeping willow and said it looked like two hands folded in prayer.

I have seen a hand pointing upward and winged deathheads
a stone saying "Once I was walking above ground like you . . . "
and a bass boat engraved on a headstone.

A poet was presented with two vases from her apartment buiding basement and once the haunting started she realized they were cremation urns. She wants a whole bone from her mother. A man opened up the bag of a great wizard's remains and gave a handful to a friend. She is now upset at the thought of dividing the ashes:

her brother wants to keep them in an urn while she wants to scatter them into a body of water.

You wanted a headstone as evidence
we have no children

I have only
the poet's arsenal
words
with which to build this
hope chest.

Allen Ginsberg's shoe shine kit, wooden box, and the white ceramic dove that a fan had sent him (things that Sotheby's couldn't sell at his estate auction).

Larry Rivers's boots with paint splotches (stolen by his lover, our friend).

My great-grandpa's pocket watch (gift from grandma).

My father's tobacco pipes (divied up among his children even though he died of emphysema).

A formal studio photograph of two nuns bought at a Kentucky auction. The nuns are in full habit and around their waists they wear the thickest rosaries: fat, wooden beads, with a christ figure hanging from the rosary tail.

Portrait of a hound dog, done in oils and in a gilt frame. First pick in a thrift shop, I arrived minutes after the loved one's family dropped a load off. The painting has darkened quite a bit; not much light left in it, the background black and the dog brownish red.

Sugar bowl, swan on lake scene, with missing lid, from estate auction of our family druggist. Also the orange Czech platter which I served you from.

Surely this metal filing cabinet once belonged to someone once who is now, do I really need to say it?

There are too many persons, places, and things.

I'll never be able to take them all.

This living noun, Charlie (age eighty-six), complains that he has no one left but two sisters in Italy. His girlfriend, whom he should have married, died a while back, and he walks and lives alone and complains of misery.

A three-foot-long group portrait of United Spanish War Veterans, Cleveland, Ohio, September 24, 1917. Every edge torn. The provenance: St. Vincent de Paul thrift shop.

A sketch of a ship and a televison set from my husband's grand-mother.

Stereoscope and cards (belonged to my grandma). Spent the evenings viewing *Milking the Goats, Hardanger Fjord Norway*, endlessly fascinated by the forms of entertainment before television came along.

Some people say I have too much stuff. They don't realize how much more I could have.

I can only say "objects of the earth, objects of the earth."
I plan to leave some nail clippings by the bed and some hairs on the pillow.

So embarassing. Thank goodness I'll be dead.

The city dump is my memoir thus I never lose sleep knowing these objects will never leave the earth.

SOURCES

Page 23: *Underground Railroad, The Invisible Road to Freedom Through Indiana,* as recorded by the Works Progress Administration Writers Project, Indiana Department of Natural Resources, Division of Historic Preservation and Archaeology, 2000

Page 23: *The Underground Railroad, As it Was Conducted by The Anti-Slavery League,* Col William M. Cockrum, J.W. Cockrum Printing Company, Oakland City, IN, 1915.

Page 25 and 28: *Report to Indiana Department of Natural Resources, Division of Historic Preservation and Archaeology, Concerning Underground Railroad Activity in Southwestern Indiana,* Dr. Randy Mills, Mark Coomer, Leslie Coomer, Sandy McBeth, Indianapolis, IN, 2001.

Page 27–28: *Lyles on Lyles Station, Yesterday & Today.* Carl C. Lyles, SR. University of Southern Indiana, 2000.

Page 47: *The Harris Family of Warrick County Indiana,* Gerald and Gloria Lewis, Windmill Publications, Inc., Mt. Vernon, IN, 1995.

Page 52: *On Jordan's Banks: Emancipation and Its Aftermath in the Ohio River Valley.* Darrel E. Bigham, The University Press of Kentucky, 2006.

Page 50: 1818–1968 Rockport-Spencer County Sesquicentennial, 1968.

OTHERS

The Life of Josiah Henson: Formerly a Slave, Now an Inhabitant of Canada, Josiah Henson, Applewood Books, Bedford, Massachusetts, 2002.

Our Hoosier Heritage, Spring Station Chrisney, Indiana, 1865–1987.

Uncle Tom's Cabin, Harriet Beecher Stowe.

Bound for Canaan: The Underground Railroad and the War for the Soul of America, Fergus M. Bordewich, HarperCollins, NY 2005.

Bury Me In a Free Land: The Abolitionist Movement in Indiana, 1816–1865, Gwendolyn J. Crenshaw, Indiana Historical Bureau, Indianapolis, IN, 1993.

Colophon

The Marvelous Bones of Time was designed at Coffee House Press,
in the historic warehouse district of downtown Minneapolis.
The type is set in Caslon.

Funders

Coffee House Press is an independent nonprofit literary publisher. Our books are made possible through the generous support of grants and gifts from many foundations, corporate giving programs, individuals, and through state and federal support. This book was made possible in part, with a special project grant from the Jerome Foundation. Coffee House Press receives general operating support from the Minnesota State Arts Board, through an appropriation by the Minnesota State Legislature and from the National Endowment for the Arts, and major general operating support from the McKnight Foundation, and from the Target Foundation. Coffee House also receives support from: an anonymous donor; the Elmer and Eleanor Andersen Foundation; the Buuck Family Foundation; the Patrick and Aimee Butler Family Foundation; Stephen and Isabel Keating; the Lenfesty Family Foundation; Rebecca Rand; the law firm of Schwegman, Lundberg, Woessner & Kluth, p.a.; the James R. Thorpe Foundation; the Woessner Freeman Family Foundation; Wood-Rill Foundation; and many other generous individual donors.

This activity is made possible in part by a grant from the Minnesota State Arts Board, through an appropriation by the Minnesota State Legislature and a grant from the National Endowment for the Arts. MINNESOTA STATE ARTS BOARD

TARGET.

To you and our many readers across the country,
we send our thanks for your continuing support.

Good books are brewing at coffeehousepress.org

BRENDA COULTAS is the author of *A Handmade Museum*, winner of the Poetry Society of America's Norma Farber First Book Award. An Indiana native, Coultas now lives in New York where she is on the faculty at Touro College and teaches in the Bowery Poetry Club's Study Abroad on the Bowery program. A 2006 New York Foundation for the Arts Fellow, Coultas has also served as series curator at the Poetry Project and as a frequent instructor at Naropa University's Summer Writing Program.